Strange & Wonderful Creatures

Poems

John Palen

Sheila-Na-Gig Editions

Strange and Wonderful Creatures © 2024 John Palen

Cover photo: "Shop Window" by John Palen
Author photo: Kent Curtis Miller

ISBN: 978-1-962405-13-3

Sheila-Na-Gig Editions
Russell, KY
Hayley Mitchell Haugen, Editor
www.sheilanagigblog.com

ALL RIGHTS RESERVED
Printed in the United States of America

Acknowledgments

I am grateful to the editors of the following publications, where these poems originally appeared:

Fine Lines: "Spotting for Maple Grove"
Ocotillo Review: "Ritual"
Off the Coast: "My Father's .38"
Sleet: "So Much Depends," "Tikkun Olam"
Sheila-Na-Gig online: "A Nice Spring Rain," "Down in the Pit," "In the Destructive Element,"
Willawaw Journal: "Small Pieces Refusing," "Time and Stillness"

The quotation at the end of "Small Pieces Refusing" is by Elizabeth Cowling, to whose *Picasso: Style and Meaning*, Phaidon Press, London, 2002, I am indebted.

To Judith Kerman
Mentor, Publisher, Friend

Contents

Grizzly Bear Sow	9
A Nice Spring Rain	10
Encounter With My Father	11
My Father Takes Me With Him to Fall Market in Kansas City	12
My Father's .38	13
My Great-Aunt Lute	14
Uncle Ralph and Aunt Esther	15
In the Destructive Element	16
Woman Reading the News	17
Tikkun Olam	18
Pro Bono	19
Just One More	20
The Three Graces Under the Male Gaze	21
Ritual	22
New England Asters	23
Love Among the Penguins	24
We Moved to the Grand Prairie	25
Small Pieces Refusing	26
Announcement	27
Red Maple	28
Spotting for Maple Grove	29
Time and Stillness	30
Down in the Pit	31
Before the Crowded Hour	32
So Much Depends	33
To My Best Reader: A Love Poem	34

Grizzly Bear Sow

In fall she eats. Has to, all the time,
a manic insatiability for ground squirrels,
huckleberries, cutworm moths,
and now the drug of corn, a new crop
in this corner of Montana. Corn's rich
and easy, and she needs to put on fat,
lots of it, before winter.

Then she'll make a den for warmth and safety
high on the slope: a snow-plugged tunnel
angling up to a cramped chamber
lined with boughs and duff. For five months

in twilight sleep, she'll tick slowly over, eat nothing,
re-metabolize feces and urine to make it through.
The cubs come naked, blind, helpless,
small as moles. They'll nuzzle close,
suck her gaunt by spring.

They'll grow quickly on the mountain,
feasting on carrion, fleshy roots, young elk;
at ripening-time she'll lead them down
into the valley for apples
and the corn.

If you struggle so hard to farm
that you need to grow corn in grizzly country,
do not go in the field when it's tall.
You won't know she's there
until she's there.

A Nice Spring Rain

It's raining today, a spring rain
like the day you gave me birth.
No memory of it, only a sure
feeling I couldn't trace. Once

when I was four or five,
we sat on the screened porch
of the first house I ever knew,
and you told me: "It rained that day,

just like this, a nice spring rain."
Your voice was a low alto
and the blue, trellised clematis
caught and held the rain.

Reading today of Great Ape mothers
who hold their newborns close,
gaze long into their eyes,
I imagine how we were.

Encounter With My Father

>   *Boy Leading a Horse,* Pablo Picasso
>   The Museum of Modern Art, New York (1906)

The boy and horse stand alone,
bare on a bare plain,
a place without a story. The mare
turns to the boy as he extends
an arm to her, a loose fist,
as if he holds a bridle.

But there is no bridle;
he leads and she follows
through some irresistible force
each way between them.

If there were a bridle, there would be a story.
He would witness murder, clerk in a shop,
marry young for love—a beautiful woman—
die before his time. The horse
would go the way of horses.

My father was that boy, once,
led that horse.

My Father Takes Me With Him to Fall Market in Kansas City

Traveling salesmen crowd
the Muehlebach Hotel,
show samples in their rooms—
spring suits on wheeled racks,
shirts fanned out on beds,
pajamas and robes stacked on dressers.

My cautious father will mostly buy
what he buys for the store each autumn:
plain blue and white dress shirts
in oxford cloth and broadcloth,
short-sleeve plaids and checks,
suits in grays and muted blues
with just a thread of orange.
He orders shirts by the gross,
suits and blazers by the dozens,
spends thousands in a single day.

A sudden gleam in his eye:
"What's hot? What'll be big
next spring?" The salesman lays out
pink polos, charcoal slacks, Hawaiian shirts
with green and yellow neon fish.
"I'll take two dozen each of those,"
my gambler father says.
"See how they do."

My Father's .38

Fired into the sky each New Year's Eve,
it was his go-to-hell insurance policy
against burglars and Commies,
his role-play as a tough-guy dandy
from the town's wrong side.
When I asked where the slugs came down,
thinking they had to, somewhere,
he said no one would be hurt
who had sense enough to stay indoors.

A shrouded-hammer Smith & Wesson,
it nested in a tin box with car titles,
the mortgage and his old draft card.
Home alone, I'd play tough guy myself,
get it out, load it, spin the cylinder,
shake the bullets out in my palm.

When cancer broke in and took everything,
my bedridden father began to ask,
"Where's my gun? Where's that old gun I had?"
Mother lied until she tired of lying,
then put it in a paper sack with the box of bullets
and took them downtown to the sheriff.
When she told my father what she'd done,
he lashed out at her, which he almost never did,
and then he wept, and took her hand.

My Great-Aunt Lute

Her mother was Southern,
a blue blood who married down,
her father a rough militia colonel
who drank himself dead
soon after her christening.
They named her Lewis
for their first, a boy who died,
but everyone called her Lute. Or Lutie.
She had no choice in the matter.

Early marriage to a doctor,
no children, widowed thirty years.
Given the chance, could she have been
something, a nurse, a doctor herself?
Would she have learned to drive?
She and her sister-in law,
my profane grandmother,
shared a house; I never saw them
share a meal, hardly a word.

Tall and raw-boned in filmy dresses,
she had the money, the pedigree,
the past—tintypes and sepia photographs
of stern men and beautiful women
bound in heavy, lacquered albums.
Even before her eyesight failed
she was tired of them.

In the end she had the Cardinals,
Harry Caray calling the games on radio,
a highball with a maraschino cherry at her side.
She was there for the Golden Years:
Marty Marion, Schoendienst, Slaughter's
Mad Dash to win the Series,
Musial in his prime.

Uncle Ralph and Aunt Esther

They were kind and I loved them
and even today it seems
a betrayal to tell you

they killed one dog after another
by feeding it from their table
until its heart gave out.

Then their own hearts would break
and they would have a small stone carved
for the back-yard cemetery
and add it to the row.

In the Destructive Element

Guernica, Pablo Picasso
Museo Nacional de Arte Reina Sofia, Madrid (1937)

I saw it only once in person,
came on it unexpectedly,
in shock and silence,
the huge, stretched canvas a scream
in black, gray, and white.

I'm young, Midwestern,
first time in New York, this stricken town.
Picasso and Franco are still alive,
the painting in defiant exile here.

For days now, we've bombed Hanoi.

On 10th Avenue an ambulance
makes a broken-field, headlong dash
through stop-and-go traffic,
high-pitched siren crying
for someone, all of us.

Woman Reading the News

A laptop screen
in a darkened living room.
In its blue light, a woman's
serious, attentive face.

She's reading about children
separated from parents.
There's a photo of a mother
in blue detention scrubs.

An immigration judge
asks if she has questions.
"I have just one," she says,
"It is regarding my son."

She says she left messages
at a number she was given,
but no one calls. She asks
the judge, "Is he OK?"

The woman who is reading
reaches up with two fingers
to touch the pulse
sheltered under her jaw.

Tikkun Olam

Two asphalt patchers from the city came today
in work boots and yellow safety vests.
The man drove a slow-rolling truck
that trailed bitumen's sharp smell,
the woman tai chi'd behind with a hose,
spraying cracks in the heaved, beat-up street.

It was the first warm day of spring,
and we walked under dark branches,
bare except for the small red flowers of maples.
The woman's art, her black calligraphy,
bold strokes and swirls, drew our eyes
to the old street's brokenness, and its repair.

Pro Bono

San Francisco, February 2004

The busker knows she only has ten seconds
to hook a passer-by with something beautiful,

score some loose change in her violin case,
maybe a twenty from a Neiman-Marcus shopper.

But when the news reaches her corner,
"Gays and lesbians are getting married at City Hall!"

she gives up a day of making rent
to go play for these misfits, outsiders, aliens

guilty of love. She feels it as she climbs
the rotunda stairs and sees the crowd below

of couples with freshly issued licenses
calling out their names, how long they've been together.

Officiants and witnesses declare them legal, ordinary.
Music cascades through the air.

Just One More

It's an old crabapple,
not pruned for years,
more thicket than tree.

I cut dead and diseased
limbs and branches,
little shoots on the trunk.

After an hour I'm
tired, but see just
one more beckoning

limb—
it's healthy but
crowded, growing

the wrong direction.
I stand directly
under it, sawing,

wanting to get this
done. When it breaks
free I have one

second before it
hits me to consider
this is how soup

is ruined, relation-
ships come apart,
wars start.

The Three Graces Under the Male Gaze

The Three Dancers, Pablo Picasso
Tate, London (1925)

We stretch our pink nakedness
on the cross of your hard gaze,
contort ourselves in slit skirts,
our mouths a grimace, a red
wound. We show you our breasts,
spilled out or thrust up in silhouette
into wall-papered, blue-lit rooms.
Sometimes we even dance with you,
Death's tango, in chiaroscuro.
Our eyes never meet.

You! Hypocrite voyeurs!
It's through your eyes
as well as our own
that we see ourselves.
Look, how we all hold hands
in this savage minuet.

Ritual

> *Les Demoiselles d'Avignon*, Pablo Picasso
> The Museum of Modern Art, New York (1907)

We've forced our way in, intruded on them
in a dressing room or harem or brothel
in various degrees of nakedness.

Two stare at us, startled but passive;
two others try to do something:
open a curtain, raise an alarm.

The seated one, her body
wrenched around to glare at us
through a mask of rage,
will perform the exorcism.

She'll sever our balls
with an ivory-and-silver knife,
wash them in a river at flood
until they are bloodless and pale,

consecrate them to a terrible goddess
by braising them over hot coals
for every woman who ever lived.

New England Asters

Who knew when we bought you on impulse
and stuck you in the ground and waited
for the ragged end of fall, when coneflowers,
black-eyed Susan and goldenrod
had blossomed and dropped their petals,
and only the pungent marigolds remained,

who knew that you late bloomers would
open yourselves to this swarm of honeybees and
randy butterflies as small and brown as pennies,

and that they'd crawl all over you,
unable to leave you alone those
last warm days,
go crazy over your florets
and hairy stems and sticky places,

and turn all rotten inside
for you, babe, only for you.

Love Among the Penguins

Based on The Last Cold Place
by Naira de Gracia

It's halfway to summer on the Antarctic Circle,
a break in the world's worst weather
with temps above zero and moderate gales,
and the chinstrap penguins are making nests
from pebbles. Pebbles are all they have
and males fight over the good ones—
slap, screech, tear at each other,
tumble over the shit-covered slope

until one decides oh
never mind and the other
waddles with the rock in his beak
to where his mate
awaits him. He drops it carefully on the pile.
They face each other, stretch wide-open
beaks to the sky and croon.
She moves the rock
to a better place.

We Moved to the Grand Prairie

We moved Aunt Helen's Larkin desk,
Aunt Jen's Windsor chair, a six-foot grand piano,
footstools your Dad built with old-growth pine. We moved
walnut dining chairs bought in a Bay City thrift shop
that day he passed and we stood by the Saginaw River
thinking of him, and watched in silence its gradual
powerful seaward slide. We moved a knotty box
you helped our son build after the diabetes began
that eventually killed him. We moved a seven-foot wardrobe
bought for thirty dollars from the landlady
of the old farmhouse where we kept goats
named Golda, William, Polly, Oats and Angel,
kept a blind dog named Skaggs, pumped well water
in a yard where our children chased each other
through lush grass in the spring. We moved
seven tons of belongings with ingrained sundry
memories on a truck, saying goodbye
to a harsh north where winter loitered,
the factories' sodium lights erased the stars,
tree-farmed timber blocked horizons. We moved
where we could see all the way out to earth's curve,
where grain augers like clothes pins
fastened miles of tasseled corn to a blue sky.

Small Pieces Refusing

Portrait of Daniel-Henry Kahnweiler, Pablo Picasso
Art Institute of Chicago (1910)

I wake before dawn in pieces, light and dark
smokey facets tinged with rose. My feet,
blind moles, search the gloom for slippers;
I feel my way—adjust
the dour resting face in the mirror,
comb the inherited cowlick into a part,
select a shirt and a narrative for the day.

So I gain an assembled self, but at what risk
of lost fragments? Each is a view
from a different moment or angle,
memories that come from nowhere
when nowhere is given room:

Smell of dry grass, a phrase of Ravel,
the auditory hallucination of my father
calling me to supper across the garden at dusk.
Time flaking away. The richness of small pieces
that "refuse to lock together to produce
a clear, fixed, unitary image of the man."

Announcement

> *Self Portrait With a Palette*, Pablo Picasso
> Philadelphia Museum of Art (1906)

No more masquerades for me,
world-weary Harlequins,
sardonic winter Wanderers.
I am Picasso the Painter, 25, Iberian,

and I am done with melancholy posturing.
Whatever pain I've caused
or suffered I obliterate
with this gray wall at my back.

Humble only before my task,
sleeves rolled, I wait
for what presents itself.

Brown as desert sandstone,
I stand erect on soil
that will break me down in time,

analyze me to the last atom,
but not yet.

Red Maple

> *It is said that Red Maple is sometimes sold*
> *as Hard Maple, sometimes as Soft Maple,*
> *but never goes to market under its own name.*
> —Donald Culross Peattie

So it's left to me, the commonest tree
in North America, to celebrate myself.
I thrive in any kind of soil,
scatter seed everywhere (although
I'm state tree only in Rhode Island).

I put up with the lineman's mutilations,
the woodpecker's hammer drill, the squirrels
who wait out winter in my dead cavities.
Not famous like English Oak or Giant Sequoia,
I'm okay with being merely good

at what I'm good for: Flooring, pulp,
pallets, utility cabinets, cooking spoons,
the two-pronged pins that hold
your work clothes and underwear
up to the sun to dry.

Spotting for Maple Grove

She wakes at dawn,
makes coffee, puts off breakfast
to write her column for the paper.

The election is May 15.
Harold Acker has volunteered
to be on the council,
we need two.

Fields are pretty much dried out.
Corn is 60 percent planted.

Mae Ellis is home from the hospital.
She thanks everyone for cards and visits.

Ora Spencer fell last Thursday
and broke his hip, he is doing poorly.
The family asks for prayers.

If you missed tornado training,
there's another one May 20.

If you spot for Maple Grove
and never been to one,
you need to attend.

Time and Stillness

Seated Woman, Pablo Picasso
Musée Picasso, Paris (1920)

I knew someone just like her,
a copy editor on a daily
where I worked in the '60s.
She wore shifts, a woman
of size and almost uncanny calm,
and she wrote headlines
better than anyone I knew.
She was fast, didn't need
to count characters, just wrote
the head, which always fit,
no small thing in hot-type days.
When I struggled, she'd quip,
"The first thousand are the worst,"
and write it for me, always
accurate, on point, unforced,
straight or witty as needed.

Still, she'd encounter
a tough one sometimes
and plant a bare foot on the floor
(she often kicked off her shoes),
cross the other leg on a knee,
cradle her cheek, look into the distance
as if in a trance. While it lasted
it seemed the process of time itself,
the present ceaselessly becoming the past,
streamed through her stillness.

But she was working,
and once the head came to her,
she would stir, glance around,
type it out on a half-sheet
and stick it on the spike.

Down in the Pit

> *Three Musicians*, Pablo Picasso
> Philadelphia Museum of Art (1921)

Our chief executive wears Armani,
talks visions, missions, and goals.
The board chairman wonders
why a tuba player makes as much
as a violinist. The writhing
maestro conducts the audience
through the usual emotions;
we're lucky if he's sober
and leaves us alone.
                        And here we are,
Harlequin, Pierrot, and The Monk,
night after night in the crowded pit.
We do that spooky stuff
we've learned at such cost,
raising dead notes to life,
waiting for the rare hour

when some wild god plugs
our drop cord into the universal grid,
and even we don't understand
how we got to be so good.

Before the Crowded Hour

Acrobat on a Ball, Pablo Picasso
Pushkin Museum of Fine Arts, Moscow (1905)

The bulked-up strongman
will repeat his act tonight,
deadlift a quarter-ton barbell,
juggle 40-pound weights,
support seven rubes on a plank
across his shoulders. But for now
he's resting from the matinee
to restore his spent body.

The girl in the pale blue unitard
trains fine muscles to recall
her centering line. It runs
from divergent arms
through a small head cocked
one way, to hips cocked the other,
then down through the ball
to the world's gravity.

The Old Masters were wrong
about eternity. It's not
saints and angels in the clouds,
but these afternoons when time
stops, when force and grace,
lion and lamb hang out together
before the next crowded hour,
the 13-meter ring, 6:30 sharp.

So Much Depends

upon the young
woman on the bus
who sees a wasp

crawl the window
above my gray head
leans across

picks it off
gently
between thumb

and forefinger
and reaching up
to the open transom

lets it go

To My Best Reader: A Love Poem

I'm the only poet you read,
and then only when I
hang a poem on the fridge.
It may be days before you see it—
You're a cellist, have your hands full
with rehearsals, practicing,
intonation, shifts—but I pay
attention to what you say.
Sometimes you say, "I like it,"
and tell me what the poem means.
That's usually not what it means
to me, but I'm happy because
that's what poems do. If you say
you don't understand it, I ask you
to point to where it went bad.
If you say,"Oh, this is a long one,"
I know it's far too long, because length
is what you noticed. The good stuff
is usually near the top, so I use magic
marker to X out the bottom half.
Then we both go back to work.

Life-long Midwesterner John Palen, born in rural Missouri in 1942, worked as a store clerk, draftsman, newspaper reporter and editor, and journalism teacher. Over more than 50 years his poems have appeared in such publications as *Prairie Schooner, Poetry Northwest, Spoon River Poetry Review, Cider Press Review* and *The Formalist*, and in anthologies published by Wayne State University Press and Milkweed Editions. He won the *Passages North* Poetry Competition in 1989, was a finalist in the Howard Nemerov sonnet competition, and has been a Pushcart and Best of the Net nominee. He earned a doctorate in American Studies at Michigan State University and was awarded a National Endowment for the Humanities journalism fellowship at Johns Hopkins University. Mayapple Press brought out *Open Communion: New and Selected Poems* in 1994 and *Distant Music* in 2017. His most recent book, *Riding With the Diaspora,* won the 2021 chapbook competition at Sheila-Na-Gig Editions. He lives, writes and gardens on the Illinois Grand Prairie.

Milton Keynes UK
Ingram Content Group UK Ltd.
UKHW040022101224
452185UK00004B/264